AF270687

Dragon Boat Festival

by Grace Hansen

WORLD FESTIVALS

Abdo Kids Jumbo is an Imprint of Abdo Kids
abdobooks.com

abdobooks.com

Published by Abdo Kids, a division of ABDO, P.O. Box 398166, Minneapolis, Minnesota 55439.
Copyright © 2023 by Abdo Consulting Group, Inc. International copyrights reserved in all countries.
No part of this book may be reproduced in any form without written permission from the publisher.
Abdo Kids Jumbo™ is a trademark and logo of Abdo Kids.

Printed in the United States of America, North Mankato, Minnesota.

102022

012023

THIS BOOK CONTAINS
RECYCLED MATERIALS

Photo Credits: Alamy, AP Images, Getty Images, Shutterstock, ©Immanuel Giel p.9/ CC BY-SA 3.0

Production Contributors: Teddy Borth, Jennie Forsberg, Grace Hansen
Design Contributors: Candice Keimig, Pakou Moua

Library of Congress Control Number: 2021950543
Publisher's Cataloging-in-Publication Data

Names: Hansen, Grace, author.

Title: Dragon boat festival / by Grace Hansen.

Description: Minneapolis, Minnesota : Abdo Kids, 2023 | Series: World festivals | Includes online resources
    and index.

Identifiers: ISBN 9781098261757 (lib. bdg.) | ISBN 9781098262594 (ebook) | ISBN 9781098263010
    (Read-to-Me ebook)

Subjects: LCSH: Dragon boat festivals--Juvenile literature. | China--Juvenile literature. | Manners and
    customs--Juvenile literature. | Festivals--Juvenile literature.

Classification: DDC 394.2683--dc23

Table of Contents

The Dragon Boat Festival

The Dragon Boat Festival is an exciting Chinese holiday. It takes place on the fifth day of the fifth month of the Chinese lunar calendar. This time falls in late May or June.

The Dragon Boat Festival is celebrated throughout China and the world. People from all places can see many important elements of Chinese **culture** at the festival.

Europe
Asia
China
Africa
N
W
E
S

Dragon Boat Festival Origins

One origin story tells of an important advisor named Qu Yuan. Qu Yuan was against the ancient state of Chu joining forces with the powerful state of Qin. But the Chu emperor did not agree and **exiled** Qu Yuan.

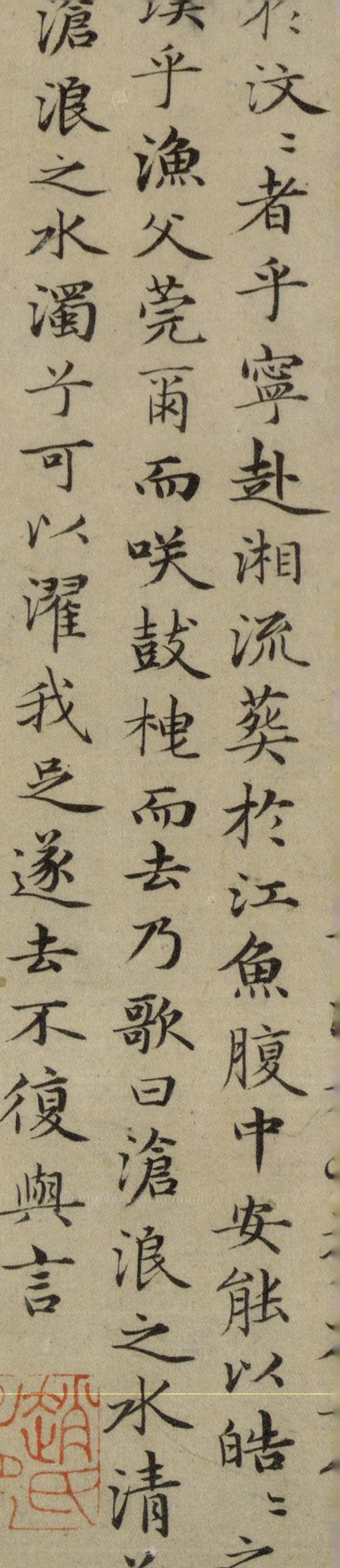

China
(260 BCE)
State of
Qin
State of
Chu
Qu Yuan

Years later, the Qin overtook the capital of Chu. Qu Yuan was so upset by the news that he drowned in the Miluo River. According to the early Han **dynasty**, Qu Yuan then became a water spirit.

中国邮政 CHINA
屈原
1.20 元
2018-15
悲歌离骚
(2-1)T
1.20 元
屈原
CHINA 中国邮政
2018-15
求索问天
(2-2)T

For centuries, supporters of Qu Yuan fed his spirit by throwing rice into the river. But a water dragon ate the rice instead. So, Qu Yuan asked the people to wrap the rice in leaves and **bamboo** stalk. This way the dragon could not eat it.

Dragons are very important
creatures in Chinese **culture**.
They are often linked to water.
This is why dragon boats have
been used by the Chinese for
hundreds of years.

The Festival Today

The dragon boat racing celebration linked to Qu Yuan began in the 5th or 6th century. Today, festivalgoers still celebrate by watching or joining a dragon boat race.

A traditional food found at the festival is zongzi. It is made by wrapping rice, meats, and beans in **bamboo** or reed leaves. It is formed in a triangle or rectangle shape. It is then tied with string.

The boat race is the most important part of the festival. The wooden boats are shaped and decorated like a Chinese dragon. Each boat can fit 30 to 60 rowers.

4
2
1
100M
21

A Dragon Boat Up Close

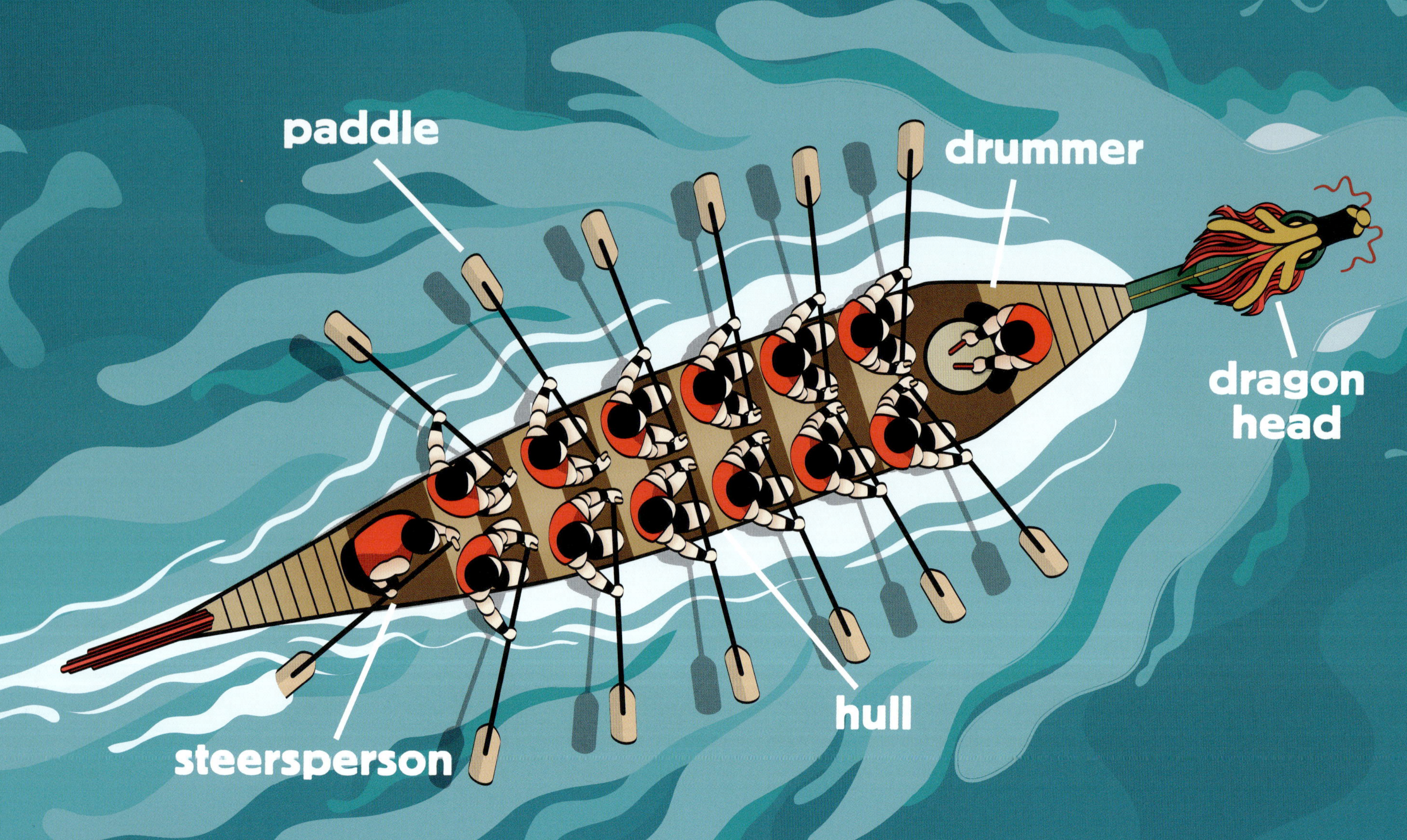

Glossary

bamboo – a tropical grass plant that has hard, woody, hollow stems.

culture – the language, customs, ideas, and art of a particular group of people.

dynasty – a series of rulers from the same family or group.

exile – sent away from one's country or home as a punishment.

Index

Abdo Kids ONLINE
FREE! ONLINE MULTIMEDIA RESOURCES

Visit **abdokids.com** to access crafts, games, videos, and more!